Wi

by Roger Phillips

assisted by Martyn Rix
and Jacqui Hurst

Elm Tree Books   London

INTRODUCTION

Aim

Here are displayed 98 of the commonest, most beautiful or interesting seaside or coastal flowers found in the British Isles and northern Europe.

How to use this book

The plants are arranged roughly in order of flowering, from spring to autumn. One photograph shows the most important parts of the plant, laid out so that details can be seen easily and clearly. The other shows the plant growing and gives some idea of its habitat, height, bushiness and stiffness. Sometimes, two closely related or similar species are shown together, and the distinctions between them are mentioned in the text.

What is a coastal plant?

Most of the plants shown here normally grow within sight of the sea. Most, in Britain at least, are exclusively maritime but some, such as Buck's Horn Plantain (page 24), are found also in sandy places inland or in inland saline areas. Other plants, such as Marsh Mallow (page 128) do not necessarily grow in salty ground but are nearly always found near the coast.

There are several reasons why plants grow close to the sea. Some like Glasswort (page 120) can tolerate, or even needs, regular immersion in salt water at high tide and so grow where other plants cannot. Others get protection from frost; Sea Spleenwort (page 14) is particularly sensitive to frost and always seems to grow near the high tide mark, and the naturalized, South African Hottentot Fig (page 126) is also confined, in Britain, to the south and west coasts. There are five main types of habitat on the coast – sandy beaches and dunes, shingle, salt marshes and estuaries, sea cliffs,

Thrift and Sea Campion on the cliffs in May, at Newgate, Pembrokeshire

and dune slacks, the damp, mossy hollows behind and between sand dunes. Each has its own special flowers. The British Isles, thanks to the warming influence of the Gulf Stream, have a very diverse selection of seaside plants. Some, such as the Oyster Plant (page 138) are found only in the north of England, Ireland and Scotland but are also found all round the Arctic. Others, such as Spring Squill (page 6) are characteristic of the western coast of Europe, as far south as Spain, and others such as Sea Stock (page 100) are really Mediterranean plants and just reach the southern English coast.

Seaside plants are also found inland, especially on mountains. Sea Buckthorn (page 130) thrives on glacial moraines in the Alps, and Thrift (page 48), Sea Campion (page 16) and Scurvy-grass (page 26) may be found growing together on some Scottish mountains. Alpine plants, such as Purple Saxifrage, often grow at sea level on the north and west coasts. The cool, wet seasides have a similar climate to high mountains. One relatively new phenomenon which has caused seaside plants to grow inland is the salting of roads in winter. The salt kills the normal plants but some seaside plants thrive, and the Sea Grass *Puccinellia distans* (page 74) and Orache (page 152) can form a dense sward in this narrow, man-made salt marsh, many miles inland.

The photographs

The studio photographs were taken on a Bronica 120 format with a 75mm lens. Scale: O is 1cm. The field photographs were taken on a Nikon FM camera with a 50 mm lens, occasionally with close-up attachments. The film was Kodak Ektachrome 64 ASA in both cases, but when used outdoors it was pushed one stop in development.

Glossary

apomitic	a plant in which seeds are formed without normal fertilization taking place: the progeny are all genetically identical to the mother plant
bract	a modified leaf beneath a flower head, or at the base of the flower stem
calyx	outer, usually green, parts of the flower
corolla	inner, usually coloured parts of the flower
obovate	ovate but broader above the middle
panicle	a branched inflorescence, often of a grass
pedicel	flower stalk
petiole	leaf stalk
pinnate	with leaflets on either side of a central stem
raceme	an elongated spray of flowers
sessile	of a leaf or flower with no stalk
spathulate	shaped like a narrow spatula
style	central part of the flower which receives pollen
umbel	many stems arising from same point, forming flat-topped head of flowers

Danish Scurvy Grass in Cornwall

Stalked or Danish or Early Scurvy-grass

Cochlearea danica (Cabbage family) is a small, overwintering annual found commonly in shingly or sandy places or on cliffs around the coasts of the British Isles; it is most common in the south west. Its usually prostrate stems radiate out from a central rosette of long-stalked, heart-shaped leaves, and may reach 20 cm long. The flowers may be white or pale purple and open in January in warm places, remaining till June in the north.

Early Scurvy-grass may be distinguished from the other species (page 26) by its long-stalked upper stem leaves, and smaller flowers, usually less than 5 mm in diameter. It has also been found inland, on ballast on railway lines, probably where the gravel originated from the shore, and along roads which are heavily salted in winter.

4

Cochlearia danica

Spring Squill (with English stonecrop) in Pembroke

Spring Squill and Autumn Squill

Scilla verna (Lily family) is a dwarf bulbous plant found most commonly in
the short turf on sea cliffs in the west and north of the British Isles, and on
the Atlantic coasts of the Faroes, Norway and France, south to Portugal.
In Ireland it is found only on the east and northeast coasts. The small
violet-blue flowers appear in April and May, in flat-topped heads of up to
twelve on rather thick stalks about 5 cm tall, after the flat (2 to 4 mm wide)
leaves have developed.

The Autumn Squill, *Scilla autumnalis*, is a Mediterranean plant found
only in dry places in the southwest, with isolated records on the Isle of
Wight and around the Thames estuary. It flowers in August and September, putting up a tall (up to 25 cm) slender stem with an elongated
inflorescence of blue to pinkish flowers. The leaves (1 to 2 mm wide)
appear after the flowers.

Scilla verna showing extremes of size

Romulea bulbocodium in Spain near Ronda

Bermuda Buttercup and Sand Crocus

Both these species just survive in the warmest parts of southwest England, but are common in the Mediterranean. Bermuda Buttercup, *Oxalis pes-caprae*, is a native of South Africa but has become established as a weed in the Scilly Isles' bulb fields and in Devon and the Channel Isles. It flowers from March to June and spreads by means of numerous bulbils.

Sand Crocus, *Romulea columnae* (Iris family), reaches the northernmost point of its distribution in one locality in south Devon but is commoner on the Channel Isles and on the coast of Brittany southwards to the Mediterranean, growing in sandy, grassy places near the sea. The tiny, crocus-like flowers open only on sunny days from March to May; they grow on short green stalks and are thus easily distinguished from true Crocuses. The larger flowered *Romulea bulbocodium* (shown here) is found commonly around the Mediterranean.

Oxalis pes-caprae near Gibraltar

Alexanders in Cornwall

Alexanders

Smyrnium olusatrum (Celery family) is a handsome celery-like biennial which flowers early and is found usually within sight of the sea in hedgerows and at the foot of old walls, around most of the British Isles except the far north. From Roman times, until the 18th century, it was grown as a vegetable, and so is often found inland, especially round medieval castles, monasteries and old buildings. The shining green leaves appear in January, and may be completely killed off by cold weather in February. Alexanders is a native of the Mediterranean regions, hence its Latin name *Smyrnium*, from the neighbourhood of Smyrna, today Izmir, in western Turkey.

It is said that the cultivation of Alexanders ceased in favour of celery; unjustly, because flowering stems, picked just before the flowers open, peeled and boiled have an excellent myrrh-like flavour, served with butter like Asparagus.

Smyrnium olusatrum

Three-cornered garlic in Cornwall

Three-cornered Garlic

Allium triquetrum (Lily family) is only hardy enough to survive in warm places along the south and west coasts of England and around Ireland, generally in hedges and by roadsides where it has escaped from cottage gardens. It is a native of the Mediterranean region, from Italy and Tunisia westwards. The rather soft flat leaves appear in autumn, the flowers in April. Three-cornered garlic can be distinguished easily from most other species by its triangular stem and nodding, bluebell-shaped flowers. The only similar species which is also naturalized is *Allium paradoxum* from the Caucasus; it usually has an inflorescence with numerous bulbils as well as one to four or more rounded white flowers, but there are forms without bulbils in cultivation. It is found mainly in East Anglia and in southeastern Scotland.

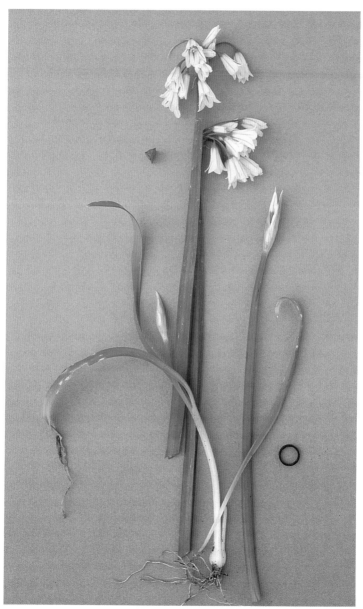

Allium triquetrum

Sea Spleenwort in Cornwall

Sea Spleenwort

Asplenium marinum is the only really maritime fern found in the British Isles. It grows in crevices on sea cliffs just above the splash zone, but is often drenched with salt spray. It is found around the British Isles from Dorset westwards and as far north as North Yorkshire. It is absent from the rest of the coast, partly for lack of suitable cliffs, but partly because it is very sensitive to frost and so cannot survive in areas with exceptionally low winter temperatures. It seems to require the extra warmth of Gulf Stream water, and is rarely found more than 30 metres above sea level.

The new fronds appear in spring and are usually from 15 to 20 cm long, but may reach 30 cm. They are evergreen, and thick and rather fleshy in texture.

Asplenium marinum

Sea Campion at Dungeness, Kent

Sea Campion

Silene maritima (Carnation family) is very common all round the coast of
the British Isles on sea cliffs or shingle beaches, and more rarely on sand
dunes. It is also found on mountains and high-altitude lake shores in
Scotland, the Lake District and Wales. The non-flowering stems are
completely floppy and lie along the ground, radiating from a stout
perennial rootstock. The greyish leaves are thick and fleshy. The flowers
appear in May on stems up to 15 cm tall, and may be found throughout the
summer, but reach their peak of flowering in June. The flowers may be
male, female, or hermaphrodite, and are often infected with a smut fungus
which causes the pollen to be replaced by blackish spores which stain the
flowers a dirty purplish-grey. When seeds are formed they can be dispersed by being blown along, trapped inside the inflated calyx.

Silene maritima

Sea Kale at Dungeness, Kent

Sea Kale

Crambe maritima (Cabbage family) is commonly found on shingle beaches just above high water in southern England, but is rare in Scotland and Ireland. It is less common on sandy beaches and on chalk cliffs. The plants form a deep branching root which can become almost woody, and have several large crowns. Succulent greyish shoots appear in April, like fat broccoli, and make a large branching inflorescence of sweet-smelling, creamy white flowers. The flowers open from June to August and the swollen single-seeded pods remain attached to the dead inflorescence. The whole may break off and be blown along by autumn gales, or float in the sea and be carried along by the tide. Sea Kale is often cultivated as a vegetable. The young shoots of established plants may be blanched by covering them with a pot, or else young plants, grown from root cuttings, may be brought indoors and forced for use in winter.

Crambe maritima

Erodium maritimum on the Lizard, Cornwall

Sea Storksbill

Erodium maritimum (Geranium family) is, like the Spring Squill, confined to the Atlantic coast of Europe and usually found from Hampshire to Lancashire, in Ireland along the south and east coasts, and on the Isle of Man. There are isolated records from Beachy Head in Sussex, and from the Mull of Kintyre and in one or two places inland. The plant is a small annual, forming a dense rosette of deeply lobed, but not pinnate leaves, with white hairs on both sides. The flowers appear from May onwards and are very small, with petals less than 4 mm long, or often absent altogether.

Other Storksbills are common near the sea, and have larger flowers, long branched stems and pinnate leaves. They are often found on sand dunes, and may be covered with sand grains which stick to their glandular hairs. Shown here is *E. cicutarium* subsp. *bipinnatum,* (syn. *E. glutinosum*) found scattered along the south and west coasts of the British Isles.

Erodium cicutarium subsp. *bipinnatum* in Kent

Wild Cabbage near Dover, Kent

Wild Cabbage

There is much doubt as to whether *Brassica oleracea* arrived in Britain by natural means after the ice age, or whether it was introduced by man as a vegetable. It is most likely to be native on the chalk cliffs from Kent to Purbeck and on the limestone from Purbeck to North Wales, but at Dover it may well have been introduced by the Romans who were great cabbage eaters, and were long established on the site of Dover Castle. It has certainly been wild at Dover since 1551 when it was recorded there by the botanist Turner. Other cliff sites for 'wild' cabbages are probably escapes of broccoli or cabbages from gardens, dispersed and fertilized by nesting sea birds, and quickly reverting to wild-looking plants. The wild plants form a stout perennial stalk, surmounted by a rosette of wavy bluish fleshy leaves. The inflorescence elongates in spring and flowers from May onwards.

Brassica oleracea

Buck's-horn Plantain

Buck's-horn Plantain

Buck's-horn Plantain, *Plantago coronopus* (Plantain family), is found usually in dry sandy places, in short turf and on cliffs all round the coast of the British Isles. It is also found inland in sandy areas such as the Breckland, the New Forest and Surrey. It is easily recognized by its deeply divided leaves in a flattened rosette, and rather short spike, 0.5 to 4 cm long, of flowers which open from May to July. It is usually a biennial but may sometimes be annual.

The Sea Plantain (see page 132) is a taller plant with narrow unlobed leaves and longer spikes of flowers.

Plantago coronopus

Cochlearia officinalis in Cornwall

Common Scurvy-grass and Long-leaved Scurvy-grass

Scurvy-grasses were so called because, as recorded by Captain Cook, they were used by sailors as a source of vitamin C, invaluable against scurvy after a long voyage. Common Scurvy-grass, *Cochlearia officinalis*, is a biennial or perennial, common around the British Isles, in salt marshes, and on sea cliffs, especially where sea birds nest, and on mountains inland. A similar species, but with a different chromosone number, *C. pyrenaica*, is found on limestone inland in Yorkshire and Lancashire. The plants are usually much-branched, up to 50 cm tall and the lowest leaves are heart-shaped. The flowers are sweetly scented, and open from April onwards.

Long-leaved Scurvy-grass, *C. anglica* (Cabbage family), is commonest in muddy estuaries in the south and up the east coast. It is recognized by its basal leaves which taper into the stalk, and by its large petals 5 to 7 mm long.

Cochlearia anglica in Essex

Sedum anglicum in Cornwall

English Stonecrop and Wall-pepper or Yellow Stonecrop

English Stonecrop, *Sedum anglicum* (Crassula family), is a characteristic plant of seaside cliffs in the west of the British Isles, but is also found on stone walls, in short rocky turf, and in south and eastern England on stabilized shingle and fixed dunes. It is almost entirely confined to acid soils and is absent from chalk or limestone areas. The non-flowering stems make a low mat of very fleshy leaves, which are greyish or often bright red in colour. The flowering stems reach a height of at most 10 cm.

Wall-pepper, *Sedum acre*, is very similar but has yellow flowers and green rather than grey leaves. It is common throughout the British Isles, on old walls and rock on limestone soils, and is often found on sand dunes or shingle.

Sedum acre

Prostrate Broom at Dungeness, Kent

Broom
Cytisus scoparius (Pea family) is not confined to the coast, but is found on acid soil throughout the British Isles and in western Europe. There are, however, special forms that have arisen in exposed seaside habitats, with either spreading or completely prostrate stems. One form with very silky leaves and prostrate stems has been called subspecies *maritimus*, and is found on cliff tops in Cornwall, Wales, southwest Ireland and the Channel Isles. Less strictly prostrate forms (var. *prostratus*) are found on shingle in Kent, forming spreading bushes about 1 metre high and 3 metres or more across. It flowers in May and June.

Cytisus scoparius subsp. *maritimus*

Sea Sandwort at Ayr, Ayrshire

Sea Sandwort

Honkenya peploides (Carnation family) is common all round the British Isles. It is often one of the first colonists of sandy beaches, where it may form small hummocks, and is also common on fine shingle. The plant is a perennial and forms spreading mats of shoots up to 1 metre across from a many-branched underground stock. The bright green, fleshy leaves have a sharp taste and were formerly used in pickle. The flowers are rather insignificant, with thin greenish-white petals on short stems up to 10 cm, and appear from May to September. The capsule is large, up to 8 mm in diameter and contains six large seeds. The plant itself can survive short periods of immersion in sea water.

Honkenya peploides

Sea Radish in Brittany

Sea Radish

Raphanus raphanistrum subspecies *maritimus* (Cabbage family) is found around most of the British Isles, but is commonest in the south and west, and absent from most of northern Scotland and eastern England. It grows on sandy or rocky shores or shingle along the drift line and on sea cliffs.

It is biennial or perennial with erect stems up to 80 cm, thinly covered with bristly hairs, and flowers from June to August. It can be distinguished from the garden radish by its flowers (usually white or purple in the garden radish) and by its fruits which are constricted between the seeds rather than spindle-shaped.

The wild radish, subspecies *raphanistrum*, is very similar, but has flowers variable in colour but rarely yellow, and fruits which break easily into one-seeded joints, with a longer slender beak. It is a common weed, particularly of acid soils.

Raphanus raphanistrum subsp. *maritimus*

Sea Rocket at West Wittering, Sussex

Sea Rocket
Cakile maritima (Cabbage family) is a pretty Stock-like (see page 100) annual found along the drift line on sandy beaches all round the British Isles; it has also been recorded on shingle.

The stems are many-branched, reaching 45 cm high. The leaves are thick and fleshy, irregularly divided, and completely without hairs. The flowers appear from June to August and vary in colour from white to pale mauve. The seed pods are irregularly shaped, very pithy, with few seeds, and can be dispersed by the tide.

In the north of Scotland, Shetland and the Outer Hebrides, Sea Rocket has undivided leaves and no teeth on the lower joint of the fruit. This variety tends somewhat towards *Cakile edentula*, a species from the Faroes, Iceland and Arctic Russia.

Cakile maritima

Trifolium scabrum at Littlestone, Kent

Rough Clover and Sea Clover

Many rare clovers are found in sandy places, by the sea, in southern England. Rough Clover, *Trifolium scabrum* (Pea family), is one of the more common, occurring from southeastern Scotland round the coast to North Wales, in eastern Ireland, and in places inland, especially on the sandy soils of the Breckland in East Anglia. It is an annual, up to 20 cm long, straggling through the grass, and flowering from May to July.

Sea Clover, *Trifolium squamosum*, grows in turf near the sea, and is especially common around the Thames estuary, around the Bristol Channel and up the Severn. Otherwise it is scattered along the east and south coasts. Its stems reach 40 cm. Its leaflets are narrowly obovate and the pink flowers which open in June and July are in a short-stalked head. The teeth of the calyx spread apart in fruit.

Trifolium squamosum

Trifolium striatum near Bordon, Hampshire

Hare's-foot and Soft Clover

Hare's-foot, *Trifolium arvense* (Pea family), is a common plant of sandy soils throughout the British Isles. It is found all round the coasts except in north and west Scotland, and is very common inland in East Anglia, Surrey and the New Forest, and other large areas of sandy soils. It is an annual, up to 20 cm, usually upright with spreading branches. The very soft woolly flower heads are easily recognized, and appear from June to September.

Soft Clover, *T. striatum*, is found in sandy places, most commonly around the coast, but also inland. It is known as far north as southeast Scotland and in Ireland it is found only on the east coast. Its stems are prostrate; its leaves softly hairy, and it flowers from May to July.

Other very small species of clover are also common by the sea. Three, *T. suffocatum*, *T. ornithopodioides* and *T. subterraneum* have whitish flowers hidden among the leaves. A fourth, *T. glomeratum*, has purplish flowers but in globular heads, and has smooth leaves.

Trifolium arvense

Restharrow at Sandwich Bay, Kent

Restharrow

Ononis repens (Pea family) is an attractive perennial, common on sand dunes, in rough grass and in dry, chalky or sandy places inland. It is found commonly all round the coasts of the British Isles, except in western Ireland and northwest Scotland where it is rare.

The stems creep and root at the nodes and are often covered with sand, which is attached to the sticky glandular hairs; flowering is from June to September.

Small Restharrow, *Ononis reclinata*, is much rarer, and confined to one or two seaside localities in south Devon, South Wales and the Channel Isles. It is an annual up to 8 cm tall, with glandular leaves, smaller flowers (less than 7 mm long), and deflexed seed pods.

Ononis repens

Gorse near Falmouth, Cornwall

Gorse

Ulex europaeus (Pea family) is found throughout the British Isles, but in Europe it is definitely more common along the Atlantic coast, being intolerant of very cold dry winters, which can kill it to the ground. It has, however, great powers of regeneration, both after frost and heath fires. Its sweet-smelling flowers may be found open for most of the year, but reach a peak in April. The pods burst in summer. Two other species are found in the British Isles. *U. gallii* is commonest in the southwest and in Wales, flowering from July to September and seeding in spring. It is usually smaller than *U. europaeus*, with very short bracteoles, 0.6 mm long. *U. minor* is more eastern in distribution in England, but otherwise is rare, and absent from Scotland and Ireland. It differs in being smaller, with shorter spines, and flowers of less than 10 mm, which have straight wings the same length as the keel.

Ulex europaeus

Horned Poppy at Sandwich Bay, Kent

Yellow Horned Poppy

Glaucium flavum (Poppy family) is a biennial or perennial found on shingle and less often on sandy beaches and cliffs. The leaves are thick and bluish with bristly hairs. The flowering stem may reach 90 cm in height; the yellow flowers may be found from June to September. The long, thin, curved pods are very striking. The Horned Poppy is common around the southern coasts of the British Isles from the Wash to southwestern Scotland, and the east coast of Ireland, but rare elsewhere.

A red-flowered species, *G. corniculatum*, is found in the Mediterranean region, and has often appeared around ports in England as a casual weed.

Glaucium flavum

Armeria maritima

Thrift or Sea Pink

Armeria maritima (Plumbago family) is one of the most characteristic and beautiful of coastal flowers. It grows on cliff tops and ledges, in salt marshes and in short turf, all round the British Isles. It is also found on mountains in Scotland, northern England, Wales and Ireland.

The plant usually makes a dense cushion, from which rise the softly-hairy stems, 5 to 30 cm tall, flowering from April to October, but mostly in May. The flowers vary in colour from deep pink to white, but are usually pale pink.

There is an inland subspecies, subspecies *elongata*, with a completely smooth flowering stem up to 50 cm. It is found in sandy places near Ancaster in Lincolnshire, and eastwards across northern Europe.

Thrift is one of the major constituents of the vegetation of cliffs colonized by sea birds, and can tolerate and even thrive on the frequent trampling and guano from the birds.

Thrift in Cornwall

Snow-in-Summer in Cornwall

Snow-in-Summer or Dusty Miller

Many alpine or Mediterranean garden plants thrive in the relatively warm and well-drained seaside soils, and *Cerastium tomentosum* (Carnation family) is a common and conspicuous example. It is a native of sunny sub-alpine rocks in Italy and Sicily, but is now widely naturalized along the coast, especially where it has escaped from cottage gardens. It is also recorded from scattered localities inland.

The leaves are white with a dense covering of fine woolly hairs, and the many-branched stems soon make a dense mat. The flowering stems are 15 to 30 cm long, and appear in May. The flowers are 12 to 18 mm in diameter, with bifid petals.

The native **Field Mouse-ear Chickweed**, *Cerastium arvense*, is rather similar, but has green and downy but not white, woolly leaves. It is found mainly in eastern England and Scotland, most commonly on chalk, but also on dunes, shingle and sea cliffs. In Ireland it is rare, being found mainly near Dublin and around Galway Bay.

Cerastium tomentosum

Diplotaxis tenuifolia in Dover, Kent

Wall Rockets

Both these Wall Rockets are found in many places inland, especially in southern England, but are most common near the sea, on sandy roadsides and in waste places.

Diplotaxis tenuifolia (Cabbage family) is a perennial, with much branched, flowering stems 30 to 80 cm high, completely without hairs. Its petals are 8 to 14 mm long, and its fruits 20 to 60 mm, on stalks almost as long as the fruit. It is not found in Ireland, and in Scotland is only known in the southeast.

D. muralis is usually a smaller, more delicate plant, an annual or biennial, with stems 15 to 50 cm high, a few stiff hairs towards the base. Its petals are 5 to 8 mm long, and its fruits 30 to 45 mm, spreading, on stalks shorter than the fruit. It is rare in Ireland, and found only in a few places in Scotland, mainly in the east.

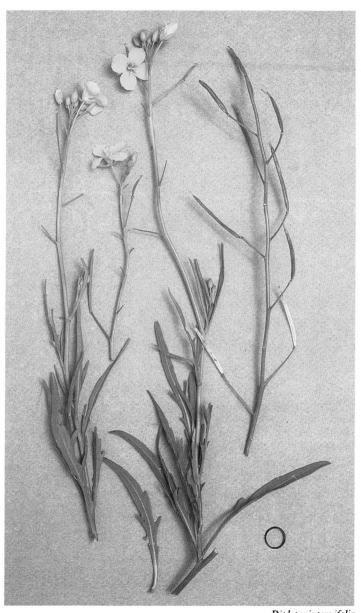

Diplotaxis tenuifolia

Sagina maritima on the Lizard, Cornwall

Knotted Pearlwort and Sea Pearlwort

Knotted Pearlwort, *Sagina nodosa* (Carnation family), is a very pretty dwarf plant found frequently in dune slacks, by lagoons or in other damp places near the sea, all round the British Isles. It is also common inland on limestone in northern England and western Ireland. It is usually about 2 or 3 inches high, with characteristic dense tufts of leaves at intervals up the stem. The white flowers are up to 1 cm in diameter.

Sea Pearlwort, *Sagina maritima*, is a minute, usually creeping plant found all round the coast in sandy places, in short turf and in crevices in rocks. It resembles the common lawn weed *Sagina procumbens*, but is an annual, and has blunt rather fleshy leaves without awns. The sepals are hooded and blunt, about equal to the ripe capsule.

Sagina nodosa at Kenfig Burrows, Glamorgan

Sea Pea at Dungeness, Kent

Sea Pea

Lathyrus japonicus (Pea family) is one of the rarest and most beautiful of seaside plants, now extinct in many places where it used to occur either because of trampling or some other disturbance to the shingle on which it grows. It is still found in East Anglia, Kent, Sussex, Dorset and the Scilly Isles, and Co. Durham, but is extinct in Wales and in Co. Kerry. In southern Scotland a narrow-leaved variety, *acutiformis*, grows on sand dunes. It is interesting that in Jutland, where both varieties are found, the broad-leaved is confined to shingle, the narrow-leaved to sand dunes.

Sea Pea is a deep-rooted, fleshy, bluish-green perennial, which flowers from June to August. The only pea likely to be confused with it is the narrow-leaved everlasting pea, *Lathyrus sylvestris*, which is sometimes also found on shingle. It has flesh-pink flowers and narrower green leaves with only one pair of leaflets per leaf.

Lathyrus japonicus

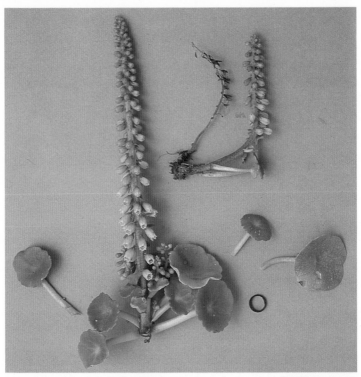

Umbilicus rupestris

Wall Pennywort or Navelwort
Umbilicus rupestris (Crassula family) is often a common feature of walls in western England, Wales and Ireland. The plant is perennial, producing its fleshy, smooth round leaves in autumn, and a stiff upright spike, up to 40 cm, of nodding tubular flowers from June to August. The leaves die off during the summer, and the plant survives the dry weather as a tuberous root. Wall Pennywort is found only along the Atlantic coast of Europe, and is absent from much of eastern England and the whole of Scotland, except the southwest. It is most common on hard acid rocks, but may also occur on limestone. It is found both inland and on sea cliffs.

Wall Pennywort in Cornwall

Sea Milkwort by the Severn Bridge, Gwent

Sea Milkwort or Black Saltwort

Glaux maritima (Primrose family) is very common in damp places all round the coast of the British Isles, usually growing in short turf, damp rock crevices, where streams enter the sea, or the upper parts of salt marshes. The stems are creeping, reaching at most 10 cm high; the smooth leaves are in four rows. The small pink flowers are stalk-less, rather hidden among the leaves, and appear from June to August. Sea Milkwort is common by the sea all round the northern hemisphere, and is often found in saline areas inland.

Glaux maritima

Red Spur Valerian in Cornwall

Red Spur Valerian

Centranthus ruber (Valerian family) is a conspicuous feature of sea cliffs or shingle in many areas, and is also commonly found inland, especially on old walls or cliffs. The seeds are ideal for colonizing this sort of habitat as they are each equipped with a parachute and can be carried along on updraughts of air.

The plant is perennial with smooth, rather fleshy, leaves and stems up to 80 cm tall. The flowers which appear from June to August may be various shades of pink, red or white. Each flower has a long spur and is pollinated by long-tongued insects, such as butterflies and moths. Red Spur Valerian is not native to the British Isles, but was introduced as a garden plant from southern Europe, probably in the 17th century.

Centranthus ruber

Sand Catchfly at Littlestone, Kent

Sand Catchfly or Striated Catchfly
Silene conica (Carnation family) is a small annual found on dunes and in dry, sandy or grassy places along the coast of southern England and the Channel Islands, and on the Breckland in East Anglia. It flowers early, from April to June, the pink petals curling up during the day. The fat, striped seed capsule is almost more conspicuous than the flower. *Silene conica* is rare in Britain, but common around the Mediterranean and in central Europe.

Nottingham Catchfly, *Silene nutans*, is also found on cliffs and shingle around the coasts of England as well as inland near Nottingham, on limestone rocks. It is a tufted perennial, with whitish nodding flowers, scented at night, on stems up to 50 cm tall.

Silene conica

Tree Lupin in Cornwall

Tree Lupin

Lupinus arboreus (Pea family) is a native of the coast of California, but has been grown in gardens in the British Isles for many years and is now found growing wild near the sea, from Scotland and Ireland to the Channel Islands. It is most common in the south and east of England.

The plant makes a rather spreading shrub up to 3 metres high, and the yellow or, more rarely, white flowers are produced from June to September in upright spikes up to 25 cm long. Tree Lupins are often killed by very cold winters, especially in gardens, but survive best on very sandy soils, and if killed, soon reappear from self-sown seed.

Lupinus arboreus

Tamarix at Sandwich Bay, Kent

Tamarix

Tamarix gallica (Tamarix family) is commonly planted by the sea in southern England, and has become naturalized in one or two places. It is native from western France to Portugal and east to the Mediterranean. It makes a feathery shrub up to 9 metres tall, covered in pale pink or white flowers from July to September. Tamarix are very easily grown from cuttings, and several other species are cultivated, some of which flower in May on shoots formed the previous year.

Tamarix gallica

Young leaves of Sea Beet

Sea Beet

Beta vulgaris, subspecies *maritima* (Goosefoot family), is very common round the coasts of England, Wales and Ireland, but is rare in Scotland and found only in the south. The plant is a tufted perennial with rather thick fleshy leaves and long sprawling, often reddish, stems with green flowers, produced in late summer. It is found commonly on shingle beaches, in the upper parts of salt marshes, or on cliffs, and is tolerant of salt spray. The leaves are edible, and make an excellent substitute for spinach. Subspecies *vulgaris* has a swollen root, and is widely planted as sugar beet, as beetroot, or in a form with wide, flattened petioles, as Swiss Chard.

Beta vulgaris subsp. *maritima*

Scotch Lovage at Whinniefold, Aberdeenshire

Scotch Lovage

Ligusticum scoticum (Celery family) is found commonly on sea cliffs in
northern Scotland and northern Ireland from Co. Down to Donegal, but is
quite absent from England and Wales. It is definitely a northern plant,
common all round the Arctic circle. The plant is perennial, with shining
leaves and, in July, umbels of greenish flowers, on stems from 20 to 90 cm
high. The leaves are aromatic, and were sometimes eaten as a herb, but are
less pungent than the cultivated **Lovage**, *Levisticum officinale*, a much
larger plant which has a strong curry-like smell.

Ligusticum scoticum

Juncus maritimus in Chichester Harbour, Sussex

Sea Rush and other Salt Marsh Grasses

Juncus maritimus (Rush family) is a very stout, clump-forming rush, found in the upper parts of salt marshes around England, Wales, Ireland and southern Scotland. Its stems may be 1 metre tall and the bract which sticks up above the flowers is very sharp. In northern Scotland and on Merseyside, *Juncus balticus*, with creeping underground stems, is found in damp, sandy places.

Sea Poa, *Puccinellia maritima* (Grass family), often forms a sward on the upper parts of salt marshes. The closely-related *P. distans* (shown here) is smaller and more tufted with reflexed branches, and is also becoming common along roadsides which are salted in winter.

Sea Couch-grass, *Elymus pungens*, is found in salt marshes and on dunes all round England, Wales and southern Ireland, but not in Scotland.

Sea Barley or **Squirrel tail grass**, *Hordeum marinum* is an annual, found in grassy fields near the sea in southeast England and south Wales, but is absent from Scotland and not known in Ireland.

Left to right: *Puccinellia distans*; *Elymus pungens*; *Hordeum marinum*

Marram grass and Dune Couch grass at East Head, Chichester Harbour, Sussex

Dune Grasses
Grasses are the most important stabilizers of sand dunes in the British Isles, and **Marram Grass**, *Ammophila arenaria*, is much the commonest. The plant creeps underground, rooting at the nodes and trapping the sand. The leaves are flat when it is wet, but curl tightly in windy or dry weather; the flowering stems reach 120 cm, with a dense panicle of spikelets up to 15 cm long in July and August.

Dune Couch-grass, *Elymus junceiformis*, is also an important stabilizer of sand, especially of the youngest dunes. The barely overlapping spikelets, and tough wiry stems and leaves are characteristic.

The **Sand Sedge**, *Carex arenaria*, is also common, with long creeping shoots under the sand, and characteristic straight lines of young plants.

Left to right: *Ammophila arenaria; Elymus junceiformis; Carex arenaria*

English Cord-grass in Chichester Harbour, Sussex

Salt Marsh grasses and rushes

The commonest grass on salt marshes is the **English Cord-grass**, *Spartina anglica*. It is a very aggressive, spreading plant forming large patches and causing silting of otherwise unstable mud. It originated in Southampton Water in 1878 as a hybrid between an American and a rather rare European species of Cord-grass, and is now found all round the coasts of England and Wales, in Scotland and Ireland, and in Europe.

Juncus gerardii, a rush, is a delicate mat-forming plant of the upper parts of salt marshes, or other damp places by the sea. It is very common all round the British Isles.

Sea Club rush, *Scirpus maritimus* (Sedge family), is common in wet places near the sea and along tidal rivers. The triangular stems are characteristic.

Left to right: *Scirpus maritimus; Spartina anglica; Juncus gerardii*

Dittander at Sandwich, Kent

Dittander or Broad-leaved Pepperwort

Lepidium latifolium (Cabbage family) is found scattered round the coast of England and Wales, and southern Ireland, especially around the Thames and Severn estuaries and in East Anglia. It is most common on old sea walls and among reeds on the edges of tidal rivers. The plant is perennial, smooth, and produces a many-branched inflorescence of tiny white flowers in June and July. The broad basal leaves may be simple or pinnately lobed.

Lepidium latifolium

Marsh Helleborine at Kenfig Burrows, Glamorgan

Marsh Helleborine and Marsh Orchids

Marsh Helleborine, *Epipactis palustris* (Orchid family), is one of the most common and most beautiful of the orchids found in dune slacks, often growing in great numbers among creeping willow. It is also found in wet fields and fens inland, but these habitats are becoming more rare whereas most dune slacks are preserved. The flowers appear from June to August; the stems are up to 45 cm high.

Many species of Marsh Orchid, *Dactylorhiza*, occur in dune slacks; they are often very striking with short stems and dense spikes of flowers. Most common is *D. incarnata* subspecies *coccinea* with deep crimson flowers, found in northern and western England, Wales and Ireland, and *D. majalis* subspecies *purpurella* with magenta flowers, common in Scotland and northern England and Ireland.

Dactylorhiza incarnata subsp. *coccinea* at Kenfig

Lizard Orchid on dunes in Kent

Lizard Orchid

Himantoglossum hircinum (Orchid family) is a very rare but striking and easily recognized orchid found in large numbers in one or two places on sand dunes in Kent and North Devon. Inland it is found mainly on the chalk in East Anglia. On the Continent it is much more common, and can often be seen by roadsides on chalk or limestone in France and around the Mediterranean. The leaves appear in winter and are usually dying before the flowers open in June and July. The stems can reach 90 cm and have numerous flowers which smell of goats.

Himantoglossum hircinum

Broomrape on Sea Holly at Sandwich Bay, Kent

Broomrapes

Broomrapes are orchid-like plants, without leaves or any green pigment, living as parasites attached to the roots of other plants. They are usually brownish or purplish, rather fleshy and covered with dense, fine hairs.

A beautiful Broomrape, *Orobanche amethystea*, is found on the coasts of Kent and southwest England and is usually parasitic on Sea Carrot or, as shown here, on **Sea Holly**.

Ivy Broomrape, *O. hederae*, is another species often found by the sea, in this case, parasitic on ivy growing on limestone cliffs. Two rare species are *O. alba*, which is usually a deep purplish-red colour, parasitic on *Thymus* in southwest England, western Ireland and west Scotland, and *O. caryophyllea*, **Clove-scented Broomrape**, parasitic on bedstraw (*Galium* subsp), and found in North Wales and on dunes in east Kent.

Orobanche amethystea

Pyrola rotundifolia subsp. *maritima* at Kenfig Burrows, Glamorgan

Round-leaved Wintergreen and Grass of Parnassus

Round-leaved Wintergreen, *Pyrola rotundifolia* subspecies *maritima*, is found in dune slacks growing among creeping willow, often making large patches and flowering very freely. It is found in several places in England and Wales from Lancashire and Anglesey to Glamorgan and North Devon, and appears to be increasing its range. The dune slack subspecies differs from the inland subspecies, in having a shorter style, 5 to 7 mm, shorter, broader calyx lobes, and shorter pedicels.

Grass of Parnassus, *Parnassia palustris*, also has a dune slack variety which has been called var. *condensata*. It is generally shorter, with more tufted stems, leathery leaves and larger flowers than the inland form which is found on wet hillsides, in marshes and on wet sea cliffs. Var. *condensata* is found scattered round the coast of Scotland, Wales, northwest England and Ireland, where similar-looking plants are also found on limestone lake shores inland.

Parnassia palustris var. *condensata* near Tayport, Fife

Cliff Sand-spurry in Brittany

Cliff Sand-spurry

Spergularia rupicola (Carnation family) is common on sea cliffs in south-western England, Wales, Ireland and southwest Scotland, but absent elsewhere. The easternmost British localities are on the Isle of Wight. On the Continent it is found from Italy along the coasts to western France. The plant is perennial, densely covered with glandular hairs all over, with numerous creeping stems up to 15 cm long, and pretty pink flowers 12 mm or more across, which open in the sun. Flowering is from June to September. The petals are plain pink, not pink with a white base as in *S. media* and *S. marina* (see page 136).

Spergularia rupicola

Slender thistle in Brittany

Slender Thistle

Carduus tenuiflorus (Daisy family) is found on sandy roadsides and other waste places near the sea. It is common around most of the coasts of England, Wales and eastern Ireland, but rarer in Scotland, and absent from the north and northwest coasts. It is an annual or biennial with winged and spiny upright stems. The flowers open from June to August, and are pale purplish red; the heads are in clusters of 3 to 10, cylindrical and less than 10 mm in diameter, which distinguishes Slender Thistle from the **Welted Thistle**, *C. acanthoides*, which has more or less spherical heads, 10 to 20 mm in diameter.

Carduus tenuiflorus

Sea Arrowgrass in Cornwall

Sea Arrow Grass

Triglochin maritima (family *Juncaginaceae*) is a rush-like plant common in salt marsh turf or damp places on sea cliffs all round the British Isles, and throughout the northern hemisphere from North Africa to the Arctic. The plant is perennial, with flowering stems up to 50 cm tall. The flowers are small, green, in a spike-like raceme which does not elongate after flowering. The flowers have six small sepals, and the developing fruits are flask-shaped on short, spreading stems. The closely-related *T. palustris* is common in marshes inland, and has club-shaped fruits appressed to the elongating inflorescence.

Triglochin maritima

Curled Dock at Dungeness, Kent

Seaside Docks

Curled Dock, *Rumex crispus* (Bistort family), is common throughout the British Isles in waste places, but its maritime variety, var. *trigranulatus*, is especially conspicuous on shingle beaches on the shore line, and in dune slacks. It can be recognized by its narrow, wavy-edged leaves and fruiting sepals 4.5 mm long, entire on the margin, with 3 equal tubercles.

Rumex rupestris is strictly a seaside plant but is much more rare, found only in Devon, Cornwall, South Wales and the Channel Islands, on sea cliffs, rocks and dune slacks. It has bluish-green leaves, a lax inflorescence with separate whorls of flowers, and small fruiting sepals 3 mm long, all with prominent tubercles.

Rumex crispus var. *trigranulatus*

Sea Carrot in Cornwall

Sea Carrot

Daucus carota subsp. *gummifer* (Celery family) is common along the coasts of Devon and Cornwall but rarer elsewhere, and often merges into the ordinary wild carrot. True Sea Carrot is found only as far east as Kent, and north to Anglesey on the Welsh coast; there are also records from eastern and southern Ireland, and the Channel Islands, both from sea cliffs and dunes. It may be recognized by its short, stout stems, and the densely bristly and hairy rays of the umbel which is convex, never concave as in inland wild carrots. It is also earlier flowering, regularly coming into flower in May.

Daucus carota subsp. *gummifer*

Sea Stock, at Kenfig, Glamorgan

Sea Stocks

Wild Sea Stocks (Cabbage family) are very rare in the British Isles but are a common feature of many coasts in the Mediterranean.

Matthiola sinuata is known only from cliffs and dunes on the west coast of England and Wales, and formerly from Ireland. It is a biennial, often large but never shrubby, and has distinctly wavy-edged leaves. The pale purple flowers which are fragrant in the evening open from June to August.

A second species, *M. incana*, is the ancestor of the cultivated annual 'Ten Weeks Stock' and the perennial 'Brompton Stock', and is usually a shrubby perennial. It is found wild on sea cliffs in southern England and the Channel Isles, particularly on the Isle of Wight. The flowers which appear from May to July vary in colour from purple to white, on stems up to 80 cm tall.

Matthiola sinuata

Sea Spurge at East Head, Chichester Harbour, Sussex

Sea Spurge

Euphorbia paralias (Spurge family) is the commonest seaside Spurge, found all round the south coast from the Wash to southwest Scotland and round most of Ireland. It is a tufted perennial with fleshy bluish-green leaves and stems up to 40 cm high. The green flowers are found all through the summer. It is found on sand dunes from the upper shore line to open places in the older dunes, usually among Marram grass (see page 76).

On the Atlantic coast, Sea Spurge is common from Belgium to Morocco, and all round the Mediterranean sea.

Euphorbia paralias

Portland Spurge in Brittany

Portland Spurge

Euphorbia portlandica (Spurge family) is found on dunes, shingle and cliff tops in western England from the Isle of Wight to southwest Scotland, and round most of Ireland, flowering from May to September. It differs from Sea Spurge in being more delicate in texture, often biennial, and in the leaves which have a prominent midrib on the under surface and end in a small sharp point.

Another species often found on old dunes, e.g. near Bettyhill in Sutherland, is the **Cypress Spurge**, *E. cyparissias*. It is native of southern Europe and is often grown in gardens. It forms large spreading patches of upright stems about 20 cm high, with very narrow leaves and yellow or often reddish bracts.

Euphorbia portlandica

Lady's bedstraw on dunes at Sandwich Bay, Kent

Lady's Bedstraw

Galium verum (Madder family) is common throughout the British Isles, in dry grassy places, but is especially conspicuous on sand dunes and sea cliffs, all round the coast. Its yellow flowers open in July and August.

Galium mollugo is also common inland, less so on dunes and cliffs. It has white flowers and broader leaves. Shown here is subsp. *erectum* which has a rather narrow panicle of flowers.

Also shown here is the hybrid between *G. verum* and *G. mollugo*, *G. x pomeranicum*, which is often found where the parents grow together. It is especially common along the south coast of England and inland on chalk and limestone. It has pale greenish flowers and leaves intermediate between the parents.

Left to right: *Galium mollugo; G. verum; G. pomeranicum*

Rosa rugosa at West Wittering, Sussex

Rugosa Rose

Rosa rugosa (Rose family) is a maritime plant in its native Japan and Korea, where it grows on sand dunes and rocky shores. In England and Scotland it has found sand dunes much to its liking, spreading underground by suckers and forming spreading patches of leathery, deeply-veined leaves. The flowers are usually deep pink, produced throughout the summer, and the large red hips are also conspicuous. At present it has been recorded from places as far apart as Wittering in Sussex, and Carnoustie Links near Dundee.

Rosa rugosa

Burnet Rose at Kenfig Burrows, Glamorgan

Burnet or Scotch Rose

Rosa pimpinellifolia (Rose family) is the most common species on dunes and on limestone rocks near the sea. It is found all round the coast of the British Isles, and more rarely, inland in sandy or limestone areas. The bristly and prickly stems are usually short, up to 40 cm high, with bluish leaves with 5 to 6 pairs of leaflets, and from May to July, creamy-white flowers 2 to 4 cm across. The hips are small and black. On the Continent the Burnet rose is most common in the north, but reaches as far south as Spain and Italy.

Rosa pimpinellifolia

Sea Bindweed at Sandwich Bay, Kent

Sea Bindweed

Calystegia soldanella (Bindweed family) forms small patches of small,
round leaves (hence the name *soldanella* after the familiar alpine *Soldanella
alpina*) on sandy shores, on dunes, and on shingle. It is found all round the
coasts of the British Isles, from southern Scotland southwards and in many
places in Ireland, especially on the east coast. The flowers appear from
June to August, and are pink or pale purple, up to 4 cm in diameter with
very short stems.

Sea Bindweed is found on suitable coasts all over the world outside the
Arctic and the tropics.

Calystegia soldanella

Sea Holly at Sandwich Bay, Kent

Sea Holly
Eryngium maritimum (Celery family) is frequent on sandy shores or shingle around the coasts of England, Wales and Ireland, but is rare in the north-east and is now extinct in most of Scotland, though formerly known as far north as Shetland. The whole plant is prickly and very blue in colour. The branching stems rise from a deep perennial tap root, and reach 60 cm high; the heads of the small blue flowers open in July and August.

On the Continent Sea Holly is found from the Baltic to Portugal, and around the Mediterranean and Black Sea.

Eryngium maritimum

Prickly Saltwort at East Head, Sussex

Prickly Saltwort
Salsola kali (Goosefoot family) is a spiny annual found on the shore line of sandy beaches, often with Sea Rocket (see page 36) and species of Orache (see page 152). It is known all round the British Isles, except in the far north of Scotland. The stems may reach 30 cm in length and are many-branched, often causing small dunes of sand to accumulate. The insignificant flowers open in late summer. It is tolerant both of immersion in sea water, and very dry conditions, and absorbs salt so that it was formerly collected and burnt to provide soda for glassmaking.

Salsola kali

Tree Mallow in Cornwall

Tree Mallow

Lavatera arborea (Mallow family) is a tall, almost tree-like biennial up to 3 metres high, with numerous large floppy leaves and small purple flowers 3 to 4 cm in diameter appearing from July to September. It is found all round the Mediterranean and up the Atlantic coast of France. In Britain it is found as a native only from Dorset westwards, and as far north as Antrim and Ailsa Craig, though commonly introduced in the south and East Anglia.

Closely related, and often planted by the sea, is *Lavatera olbia* var. *rosea* with much larger bright pink flowers on a less leafy shorter plant, which branches from the base. It is native of the western Mediterranean region.

Lavatera arborea

Marsh Samphire at Roman Landing, Sussex

Glasswort or Marsh Samphire

Salicornia species (Goosefoot family) are fleshy leafless plants, found in great quantity in salt marshes throughout the British Isles. Most are upright annuals, but one, *S. perennis*, is a perennial with creeping underground stems. All flower in August and September, when, in most species, one or two stamens can be seen appearing from the upper segments of the stems.

Glasswort is excellent to eat, boiled like Asparagus with one lot of water discarded while cooking to reduce the saltiness; when cooked the woody, inner stems separate from the outer fleshy edible tissue. It was collected and burnt to produce soda for glassmaking, as was Prickly Saltwort (see page 116).

Salicornia spp. *S. perennis* lower left

Rock Sea Lavender at Folkestone, Kent

Rock Sea Lavender

Limonium binervosum (Plumbago family) is an attractive tufted perennial of
sea cliffs, usually of chalk or limestone, or more rarely, of stable shingle. It
is found in suitable habitats all round the coasts of England (except the
northeast), Wales and Ireland, but in Scotland only on the Mull of
Kintyre. The purplish-blue flowers appear from July to September on
branched flowering stems up to 30 cm, but usually around 15 cm high.
Other closely-related endemic apomictic species are found on specific
cliffs; *L. recurvum* on Portland Bill, Dorset; *L. transwallianum* in Pembroke; *L. paradoxum* at St. David's Head and in Co. Clare; and *L.
companyonis* near Beachy Head, Sussex, otherwise only seen near Nar-
bonne in southern France.

Limonium binervosum

Sea Lavender at Chichester Harbour, Sussex

Sea Lavenders

Limonium humile and *L. vulgare* (Plumbago family) are both found on salt marshes in England, Wales and southernmost Scotland. Only *L. humile* is found in Ireland. They are perennials with leathery basal leaves, and branching spikes of small flowers, up to 30 cm high, appearing in July and August. In some salt marshes, they may be very abundant and colour the whole marsh a misty blue.

The characters which distinguish the two species can be seen in the photograph opposite; eg *L. vulgare*: stem not branched below the middle; inflorescence corymbose, the spikelets crowded into short, spreading spikelets. In *L. humile* the stem is branched below the middle; the inflorescence is not corymbose, and the spikelets are longer and more distant.

Limonium vulgare (below); *L. humile* (above)

Hottentot fig in Cornwall

Hottentot Fig

Carpobrotus edulis and *C. acinaciformis* (Mesembryanthemum family) are creeping succulents, native of South Africa, but widely naturalized in southern Europe, and on the southwest coast of England. The stems may be several feet long, hanging over rocks or walls; the leaves are triangular in section. In *C. edulis* the flowers are yellow or lilac, 8 to 10 cm across, with yellow stamens; in *C. acinaciformis* they are up to 12 cm across, red with purple stamens. The fruits are fleshy and edible, full of small seeds, hence the common name.

Carpobrotus edulis in Cornwall

Marsh Mallow on Romney Marsh, Kent

Marsh Mallow

Althaea officinalis (Mallow family) is found in ditches or damp grassy places near the coast. It is not common in England, and is usually associated with coastal marshes, such as the Wash or Romney Marsh, or with muddy estuaries such as the Avon and Severn estuaries in Gloucestershire, and around Southampton Water. It is found in southwestern Ireland, but not in Scotland. The leaves are soft and silky; the flowering stems are up to 1.3 metres high, and the pale pink flowers appear in August and September.

Althaea officinalis

Sea Buckthorn

Sea Buckthorn and Duke of Argyll's Tea Plant

Hippophae rhamnoides, the Sea Buckthorn (Oleaster family), is found in many places on dunes where it forms dense stiff bushes, covered in early winter with pale orange berries. The flowers are insignificant, the male and female on separate plants, and appear in March and April, before the leaves, which are narrow and covered, especially beneath, with silver scales. It is probably native on the east coast, planted elsewhere.

Duke of Argyll's Tea Plant, *Lycium chinense* (Nightshade family) is a small twiggy bush usually about 1 metre tall. The purple flowers appear from June to September, the single scarlet ovoid fruit from August onwards. It is native of eastern Asia, but widely naturalized, especially in the south.

Duke of Argyll's Tea Plant

Sea Plantain in Cornwall

Sea Plantain

Sea Plantain, *Plantago maritima* (Plantain family), is found usually in the upper parts of salt marshes, and in damp crevices on cliffs, and is frequent inland on high mountains and by limestone loughs in Ireland. It has upright linear fleshy leaves up to 10 mm (rarely 15 mm) wide, and a rather longer spike 2 to 6 cm long of minute flowers which open from June to August. It is a perennial and may form dense clumps.

The Buck's-horn Plantain (see page 24) is usually a smaller plant with a flat rosette of toothed leaves.

Also rather similar in general appearance is Sea Arrow Grass (see page 94) which often grows with Sea Plantain. Its larger, more widely spaced flowers make it easy to distinguish.

Plantago maritima

Centaurium capitatum in Cornwall

Century

Six species of century (Gentian family) are found near the sea in the British Isles. All have pink flowers which open in July and August.

Common Century, *C. erythraea*, is common on dunes, as well as inland. It has clusters of flowers, petals 5 to 7 mm long, and a rosette of basal leaves more than 5 mm broad.

C. capitatum is an exclusively seaside plant, common in parts of Devon and Cornwall, growing in short turf on cliff tops and dry grassy places. The stamens are inserted at the base of the corolla tube, which enables it to be distinguished from dwarf forms of Common Century, in which the stamens are inserted at the top of the corolla tube.

Two other seaside species are rarer, tall, slender plants. *C. pulchellum* has flowers each on short stalks; *C. littorale* has clustered flowers but narrow leaves.

Centaurium capitatum

Spergularia media in Chichester Harbour, Sussex

Sand Spurry

Spergularia marina (Carnation family) and *S. media* are two rather similar species both found in muddy and sandy salt marshes all round the British Isles. Both have petals which are white at the base, but in *S. media* they are 7.5 to 12 mm in diameter, whereas in *S. marina* they are 6 to 8 mm in width, and shorter than the sepals. In addition, *S. media* has broadly winged seeds, a longer capsule, 7 to 11 mm long, and is a generally more robust plant.

Spergularia marina

Mertensia maritima

Oyster Plant

Mertensia maritima (Borage family) is a northern plant, now very rare even where it was once common along the coasts of Scotland and northern England as far south as the Lake District. It is also found in northern Ireland. It grows on shingle beaches, forming creeping patches up to 1 metre across, of rather fleshy bluish-green leaves. The tubular flowers which open from May to August are purplish-pink and later turn to sky-blue.

Outside the British Isles, the Oyster Plant is found all around the Arctic in Europe, Asia and North America.

Mertensia maritima on the Isle of Arran

Rock Samphire in Corsica

Rock Samphire

Crithmum maritimum (Celery family) is a southern plant, quite common from East Anglia southwards, and up the west coast as far as the Solway Firth in southwest Scotland. It is common also around the southern half of Ireland, but rare in northern Ireland and western Scotland, and absent from the rest of the east coast.

Rock Samphire is usually found on cliffs, but also on rocks, old sea walls, shingle and sand. In some places it may be dominant in the spray zone on cliffs, as it is especially tolerant of salt. It is a bushy perennial up to 30 cm high, with aromatic leaves, formerly used as a pickle, and has greenish flowers from July to September.

Crithmum maritimum

Seablite in Chichester Harbour, Sussex

Seablite
Annual Seablite, *Sueda maritima* (Goosefoot family), is an annual, common in salt marshes all round the British Isles. It grows in company with Glasswort and *Spartina*, and may form a bushy plant up to 45 cm high, either bluish-green or reddish. The green flowers are insignificant, appearing from July to October.

Shrubby Seablite, *Sueda vera*, is a low shrub up to 1.5 metres high, common around the Mediterranean, but in Britain found only in East Anglia, Kent and Dorset where it is common along the back of Chesil Beach. It prefers to grow on shingle or sand, in contrast to Annual Seablite which grows on the softest mud.

Sueda maritima

Sea Purslane in Chichester Harbour, Sussex

Sea Purslane

Halimione portulacoides (Goosefoot family) is common in salt marshes around the coasts of England and Wales, eastern and southern Ireland, and in Scotland only on the Solway coast. It is a perennial, usually growing thickly along the edges of tidal channels, or as single plants among *Spartina*, or in a mixed salt marsh meadow, but occasionally dominant over large areas. The stems reach 60 cm first creeping and then erect. The spikes of greenish flowers are produced from July to October. Sea Purslane is good to eat: the leaves must be washed, boiled and then eaten like spinach.

Halimione portulacoides

Sea Heath at East Head, Sussex

Sea Heath

Frankenia laevis (Frankenia family) is a Mediterranean and central Asian
species found only in southeastern England from the Wash to the Isle of
Wight, and in the Channel Isles. It is a creeping perennial, forming mats
often 50 cm wide, and usually growing on the drier parts of salt marshes in
very short turf, or in the transition zone between salt marsh and dune. It is
less common on shingle or on cliffs. The flowers are less than 1 cm across,
purplish or pink, and appear from July to September.

Frankenia laevis

Sand Pansy at Kenfig Burrows, Glamorgan

Sand Pansy and Dune Gentian

Viola tricolor subspecies *curtisii* (Violet family), is a characteristic and very pretty plant of dunes along the north and west coasts of Britain, and all round Ireland. It has creeping underground stems, and grows usually in more stable dunes, among Marram grass (see page 76). The yellow flowers, often with blue markings, appear from May to July.

Felwort, *Gentianella amarella*, is a biennial found on dunes and chalk and limestone hills throughout the British Isles, flowering in August and September. The stems can reach 30 cm in height; the flowers are usually purplish in colour, but in subsp. *septentrionalis* from Scotland are creamy-white inside, purplish-red outside. Dune Gentian, *Gentianella uliginosa*, is very rare, found only in south Wales and in western Scotland in dune slacks, and is distinct in having long-stalked flowers.

Felwort at Kenfig Burrows, Glamorgan

Sea Wormwood on Isle of Sheppey, Kent

Sea Wormwood

Artemisia maritima (Daisy family) is a rather rare plant, but known around the coasts of England, Wales, Ireland and southern Scotland. It is commonest in East Anglia and around the Solent, growing in the drier parts of salt marshes or in the transition area between shingle and salt marsh. It is an aromatic, woolly perennial, with stems about 30 cm long, and small flower heads on branching stems which appear in August and September. Sea Wormwood can be distinguished from Common Wormwood, *A. absinthium*, by its smaller, slenderer flower heads.

Artemisia maritima

Atriplex littoralis on Isle of Sheppey, Kent

Orache

Species of Orache, *Atriplex* (Goosefoot family), are common annuals on most coasts of the British Isles, both on shingle beaches, waste ground along the drift line in estuaries, and in salt marshes. Oraches can be distinguished from Goosefoots, which are superficially similar and closely related, by the two large triangular bracteoles which surround the female flower and seed. **Frosted Orache**, *A. laciniata*, is the easiest to recognize, by its creeping stem and very silvery triangular leaves. *A. littoralis* is erect, with linear or oblong-linear leaves, and a long inflorescence which is only leafy at the base. *A. prostrata (hastata)* is very variable, erect or procumbent, usually with triangular or hastate lower leaves, truncate or subcordate at the base.

Atriplex littoralis (left); *A. prostrata* (right); *A. laciniata* (below)

Aster tripolium

Sea Aster

Aster tripolium (Daisy family) is a common plant of salt marshes, where it can colour large areas pale mauve in September. It is also occasionally found on cliffs. It is a perennial, with very fleshy leaves and branched stems with rather feeble Michaelmas Daisy-like flowers, from August onwards. There is a variant, which is often found in the south, growing among normal plants, without the blue ray florets, called var. *discoideus*.

The very rare **Goldilocks**, *Crinitaria linosyris*, also lacks ray florets, but is a cliff plant, restricted to limestone in Devon, Somerset, Wales and Lancashire. It is easily recognized by its tufted stems and numerous very narrow leaves.

Aster tripolium

Golden Samphire at Roman Landing, Chichester, Sussex

Golden Samphire

Inula crithmoides (Daisy family) is an uncommon plant of dry salt marshes,
cliffs and shingle; it is common around the Mediterranean, but in Britain
known only around the Thames estuary, in east Kent, around the Solent
and from there along the west coast to Anglesey. In Ireland it is found near
Dublin and along the south coast, and there is an isolated record of it on the
Mull of Kintyre. It is a perennial, with tufted stems and fleshy narrow
blunt leaves. The golden yellow flowers with short rays open from July to
September.

Inula crithmoides

INDEX

Roger Phillips has pioneered the photography of natural history which ensures reliable identification. By placing each specimen against a plain background he is able to show details that would otherwise have been lost if it had been photographed solely *in situ*. Such is the success of this technique that his books, which include *Mushrooms, Wild Food* and *Freshwater Fish,* have sold over a million copies worldwide. He is also the winner of numerous awards, including three for best produced and best designed books and the André Simon prize for 1983 for *Wild Food*.

Martyn Rix took a degree in botany at Trinity College, Dublin and then went on to Cambridge. After a further period of study in Zürich he became resident botanist at the Royal Horticultural Society's gardens at Wisley for several years. He is now a freelance writer.

Jacqui Hurst studied photography at Gloucester College of Art & Design, worked as assistant to Roger Phillips for 4 years, and is now a freelance journalist and photographer, specializing in country matters.

Other titles in this series:

Herbs and Medicinal Plants

Seashells and Seaweeds

Wild Flowers of Roadsides and Waste Places

garden and field
Weeds

native and common
Trees

common and important
Mushrooms

woodland
Wild Flowers

First published in Great Britain 1987
by Elm Tree Books/Hamish Hamilton Ltd
27 Wrights Lane London w8 5TZ

Copyright © 1987 by Roger Phillips

Cover design by Pat Doyle

ISBN 0241-12062-4
ISBN 0241-12027-6 Pbk

Typeset by Rowland Phototypesetting Ltd,
Bury St Edmunds, Suffolk
Printed in Great Britain by Cambus Litho